Clovis Crawfish
and the
Twin Sister

Clovis Crawfish and the Twin Sister

Mary Alice Fontenot and
Julie Fontenot Landry

Illustrated by Julie Dupré Buckner

PELICAN PUBLISHING COMPANY
Gretna 2007

It was early spring in south Louisiana where Clovis Crawfish lived. The south wind gently rippled the water in the bayou and twirled Clovis Crawfish's long whiskers around and around.

M'sieu Blue Jay was hopping around on the bayou bank, trying to find an acorn he had buried in the fall after it had dropped from the big oak tree.

Sometimes M'sieu Jay forgot just where he had buried an acorn. In time, the acorn might sprout and grow into a big oak tree just like the one that shaded the bayou bank.

Clovis Crawfish was keeping a sharp eye on M'sieu Blue Jay. He didn't mind if M'sieu Jay found his acorn. He just wanted to be sure the hungry bird didn't give up and look for something else to eat, like his small friends Christophe Cricket and Gaston Grasshopper.

Sosthène Snake slithered out of the bayou water toward M'sieu Jay.

M'sieu Jay forgot all about the acorn. He spread his wings and flew off in a hurry, squawking and complaining, "Chee-*ank! Chee-ank!*" Sosthène Snake slithered back into the bayou.

Lizette Lizard came crawling down and around the oak-tree trunk. Lizette was wearing her new pink polka-dot *garde-soleil,* which is the way to say "sunbonnet" in Cajun French.

"Clovis, have you seen my twin sister?" asked Lizette.

Clovis Crawfish clicked his big claws. "I didn't know you had a twin sister," he said.

"Yes, I do," said Lizette. "Her name is Lois Lizard, and we look exactly alike. No one can tell us apart. That's why I wear a pink polka-dot *garde-soleil* and she wears a blue polka-dot one."

René Rain Frog hopped up. "That's like the Cigale twins, Chicot and Coteau," he said. "They look exactly alike!"

"Right," said Clovis Crawfish. "Twins usually do look alike."

"But Clovis," said Lizette, "I'm worried because my twin sister isn't here. She was supposed to wait for me right here by your mud house."

"Don't worry, Lizette; we'll find her," said Clovis. "Our friends will help, and we'll find her in a hurry."

"Bonne idée," said René Rain Frog. "Great idea!" René gave one big jump and was ready to start the search. Andrew Armadillo came loping up. "Hey, *là-bas!*" he said. "What's going on?"

"Lizette can't find her twin sister. Will you help us find her?" asked Clovis.

"Sure, partner," drawled Andrew. "I'll do whatever you need. I can dig and I can swim, but someone else will have to tell me where. I don't see too well, you know."

"First of all," said Clovis, "let's send our flying friends to the other side of the bayou in case Lois Lizard went over there."

Clovis Crawfish lifted up his big, sharp claws and twirled his long whiskers. "Maurice!" he called. "Bertile! Denis! Denise! Léontine! Josette! *Venez-ici, tout le monde!*" which means, "Come here, everybody!" in Cajun French.

Maurice Mosquito Hawk flew in and lit on a thistle. "Maurice will be a great searcher!" said René Rain Frog. "His eyes can see in all directions."

Bertile Butterfly fluttered over to the honeysuckle vine. "If Lois Lizard is lost, she'll surely see me when I fly over," said Bertile, "since my wings are so big and colorful."

Denis and Denise Dirt Dauber lit on top of Clovis's mud house.

Bernard Bumblebee buzzed by.

Léontine Ladybug and Josette June Bug arrived to join the search. "I hope Tonise Too-loo-loo didn't scare Lizette's twin sister," said Léontine with a shudder.

"Don't worry, Léontine," said Andrew Armadillo. "If Tonise shows up, I'll use all my four feet to cover him with dirt!"

"*Allons,* then," said Clovis. "Let's go!" And all of Clovis's flying friends flew off across the bayou to look for Lois Lizard. Clovis and his other friends looked for her everywhere on the bayou bank.

The honeysuckle vine was covered with white and pale
yellow blossoms. Clovis grabbed the vine with his big
claw and shook it hard, hard. Nothing came out except
Simone Spider. She ran quickly into the tall grasses.

René Rain Frog looked under every fern frond.
Lizette Lizard crawled up the oak-tree trunk so that she could look for Lois Lizard in the Spanish moss that hung from the tree branches.

"*Ouaouaron! Ouaouaron!*" said Fernand Frog. "I can hop over the levee and see if Lizette's twin sister is over there!" With one push of his strong back legs Fernand was out of sight.

Siméon Suce-Fleur helped himself to a taste of nectar as he searched among the flowers.

Corinne Crapaud looked under the toadstools that had sprung up on the bayou bank.

All of a sudden Clovis Crawfish said, "Stop! I think I
see something blue in the muscadine vine!" Clovis
Crawfish and his friends rushed to the vine to look.

"It's my sister! It's my sister!" said Lizette.
"It's Lois Lizard!"

Sure enough, there was Lois Lizard in her blue polka-dot *garde-soleil*. "Help! Help!" she said. "I can't get loose! When I saw M'sieu Blue Jay, I hid here in the muscadine vine. I was afraid to move, and the tendrils of the vine wrapped themselves all around me. I can't get loose!"

Clovis Crawfish wiggled his whiskers and snapped his big, sharp claws. With one claw he snipped the muscadine tendrils, and Lois was free.

"You're a good friend, Clovis. *Merci beaucoup!*" said Lois Lizard. She scurried down the muscadine vine and joined Lizette on the bayou bank.

All the friends were happy to meet Lizette's twin sister, so they joined together to sing a welcome song.

BIENVENUE
Julie Fontenot Landry

Bi - en - ve-nue! Bi - en - ve-nue! Bi - en-ve-nue, ma chère.   Je

suis con-tent, con - tent de faire ta   con - nais - sance.____

Translation:
Welcome! Welcome! Welcome,
my dear. I'm so glad to meet you.

PRONUNCIATION GUIDE

Cajun French	English	Approximate English Pronunciation
Clovis		klo-VEES
M'sieu	Mister	mis-YUH
Christophe	Christopher	kree-STOFF
Gaston		gah-STONH
Sosthène		so-STEN
Lizette		lee-ZET
garde-soleil	sunbonnet	gar-so-LAY
René		ruh-NAY
Cigale	cicada	see-GAHL
Chicot		shee-KOH
Coteau		koh-TOH
bonne idée	good idea	bohn ee-DAY
là-bas	over there	lah-BAH
Maurice		mor-EES
Bertile		bare-TEEL
Denis	Dennis	duh-NEE
Denise		duh-NEES
Léontine	Leontine	lay-on-TEEN
Josette		zho-ZET
venez-ici	come here	vuh-NAYZ-ee-SEE
tout le monde	everybody	too luh mond
Bernard		bare-NAR
Tonise		toh-NEES
allons	let's go	ah-LONH
Simone		see-MONE
ouaouaron		wah-wah-RONH
Fernand	Ferdinand	fair-NONH
Siméon		see-may-ONH
Suce-Fleur	hummingbird	soos-FLUR
Corinne		koh-REEN
Crapaud	toad	kra-POH
merci	thank you	mare-SEE
beaucoup	very much	boh-KOO
bienvenue	welcome	byenh-vuh-NOO
ma	my	mah
chère	dear	share
je suis content	I'm so glad	jhuh swee konh-TONH
de faire	to make	duh fair
ta connaissance	your acquaintance	tah kon-nay-SOHNCE